1906 The Great San Francisco Earthquake & Fire

A Special Centennial Edition

By
Darrell Heppner

Bookman LLC
Publishing & Marketing

**Providing Quality, Professional
Author Services**

www.bookmanmarketing.com

And all that was left were the stone arches…

Dedication

Three years ago, Anne passed away after an eight year battle with breast cancer. She loved to read a good book, a good story, or a book well written…

Fifty years, she worked as a secretary for several insurance companies in San Francisco. She spent her lunch time and weekends perusing little bookstores looking for bargains and rare items. She happened upon two portfolios of the 1906 San Francisco earthquake and fire.

Two years before she passed away, we happened to walk through the Alameda Flea Market one Sunday in May. At the second table, she spotted a table of very interesting black boxes. We bought one of the boxes which contained over sixty 4x5 glass negatives of the 1906 San Francisco earthquake and fire including several which were tinted. (See cover). From our own library comes this book.

To you Anne, this book is dedicated. Thank you for a wonderful 34 years…

With Love,
Darrell

Golden Gate at Sunset

Introduction

Even an earthquake of this magnitude was not enough to destroy the city. Scores of victims were crushed to death or struck by falling debris. However, *hundreds* of people, the vast majority of the victims, were killed by the fires that raged out of control across the Bay Area. Only six months before the quake, the National Board of Fire Underwriters had warned that San Francisco was a major fire risk. The city government had little time to take any steps.

Even before the tremors subsided, San Francisco was already burning. Stoves and kerosene lamps overturned by the quake ignited fires all across the peninsula. More fires were touched off by downed power lines. Within minutes fires were burning out of control, not only in San Francisco, but also in hundreds of surrounding cities and towns. Within that 45 seconds of violent tremors, one of the first things to break was the city's water mains. Except near the waterfront, (where the first fires went out of control), firemen had little to no water to fight the blazes. For the next three days, everyone tried frantically, and mostly in vain, to put out those fires.

Burnt district as viewed from Twin Peaks.

One success story came from San Francisco's Italian neighborhood. Residents there poured over 100,000 gallons of wine on their roofs and staircases. These people's houses, stores and restaurants were saved from the flames and ashes that kept the fires spreading for the first 48 hours.

Others' efforts were not as successful. Some residents tried to make fire breaks by using dynamite to destroy buildings. However, many of these people were using explosives for the very first time, and the blasts they set off turned buildings into great piles of kindling wood. They did more harm than good, and started many new fires of their own.

Blowing up the Phelan Building, hoping to stop the fire.

Across the San Francisco Bay, people in Oakland watched in horror as San Francisco burned to the ground. Black smoke billowed out hour after hour, completely blocking out the sun.

Fire and smoke is seen rising from the California and Sansome Streets area.

Fire and smoke is seen rising from the 3rd and Mission Streets area.

Foreword

San Francisco is an American city like no other. The city and surrounding Bay Area feature mountain peaks, rolling hills, magnificent beaches and idyllic weather. This one unique place is the home of icons of breathtaking beauty. Scenes like the Golden Gate Bridge, The Transamerica Pyramid and Lombard Street are recognizable at a glance to millions of Americans – even though most of them have never even been there.

Panorama from Nob Hill before the fire.

Yet after three days just one hundred years ago, San Francisco looked more like Hiroshima or Dresden. In 2001 Americans were horrified to see the smoking ruin that was once the World Trade Center. It was a terrible sight, but it was just two buildings. In 1906 in San Francisco 25,000 buildings were destroyed just as quickly and just as completely.

Panorama from Nob Hill after the fire.

April 18, 2006 marks the one hundredth anniversary of the Great San Francisco Earthquake and Fire. Now 100 years later, the damage caused by this terrible event is no longer obvious to visitors. However, any long-time Bay Area resident can show you where land marks used to stand, (very few of the structures built before 1906 remain), and how that disaster shaped modern day San Francisco and the surrounding cities.

On April 18, 1906 at 5:14 AM, the ground shook violently for about one minute, but that was only the beginning of a cataclysm that lasted three days and became the worst natural disaster in our nation's history. The earthquake itself measured 8.25 on the Richter scale, hundreds of times more powerful than any of the earthquakes felt in California since. (The "World Series Earthquake" that struck the Bay Area in 1989 only measured 6.7 on the Richter scale, yet nearly 50 people were killed.)

At 8.25 on the Richter scale, the 1906 earthquake was one of the most powerful ever measured anywhere on Earth. The damage was so severe and the displacement of the Earth so great that seismologists and geologists were forced to fundamentally change their theories of the destructive potential of earthquakes and faults that cause them. In places, the ground moved as much as 18 feet horizontally.

The precise epicenter of the quake was close enough to San Francisco to be characterized as a direct hit. Nearby cities closer to the fault like San Jose and Santa Rosa sustained proportionately even greater damage. If a similar earthquake struck the Bay Area today, the damage and death toll would be incalculable.

However the earthquake itself was just the beginning of the disaster. The resulting after shocks and fires destroyed nearly everything the quake left standing. By the time the fires were finally put out three days later, 25,000 buildings were destroyed (nearly 500 city blocks), 250,000 were left homeless, and between 500 and 600 people were dead. (Some estimates place the death toll as high as 1500.) The damage was estimated at $350 million dollars in 1906, which would equate to untold billions in today's dollars.

Refugees in Lafayette Square.

After the California Gold Rush that began in 1849 and continued for years, San Francisco went from being a small sleepy port, to one of the biggest and most important cities in America. Almost all of the gold found near Sutter's Mill, and most of the silver of the Comstock Lode went through San Francisco. So much precious metal and commerce flowed through the city that a new mint to strike American coins was established there.

At any given time, from 1860 to the turn of the century, hundreds of ships from all over the world lay at anchor in the San Francisco Bay. Uncounted thousands of travelers first saw America through the Golden Gate.

Few people realize how important San Francisco had become by 1906. No one was prepared for how completely it was destroyed. The earthquake and subsequent maelstrom became one of the most important events in American history. For three days death and chaos ran rampant. Then amazingly, the people of San Francisco, struggled, rallied and then triumphantly rebuilt the city. This book tells that story, and celebrates that triumph.

Through rare photographs taken during the disaster and throughout the aftermath, "1906 The Great San Francisco Earthquake and Fire" brings all of those amazing events to life. Amazing things happened in the hours, days and weeks that followed April 18, 1906. This book and these photographs bring those times back to life in a way no other book can.

Fire looking down Sacramento Street.

Chapter One:

Before the Earthquake & Fire

Darrell Heppner
April 17, 1906

Span Francisco was booming right along with the rest of the nation in spring of 1906. Ten years of increasing prosperity which followed the depression of the mid-1890's had left a vivid mark on the city. Her silhouette was changing, filling out. San Francisco was riding the top of the boom, optimism colored all levels of the city life. It was a lively time for a lively town.

The Earth Shook, The Sky Burned
By William Bronson, 1959

Market Street alive and busy prior to the earthquake.

Darrell Heppner

On the eastern edge of Nob Hill, overlooking the commercial heart of the city, stood a massive white structure – an architectural masterpiece in the tradition of the Greek Revival – The Fairmont Hotel.

The Earth Shook, The Sky Burned
By William Bronson, 1959

The Fairmont Hotel

Darrell Heppner

The renowned Palace Hotel, the world's finest for many years, was built around a spectacular covered courtyard. The interior galleries and bay windows which looked out on Market and Montgomery Streets were equally splendid innovations.

The Earth Shook, The Sky Burned
By William Bronson, 1959

The Palace Hotel before the fire.

A view of Post Street from Market Street prior to the earthquake.

Another view of Post Street from Market Street with Montgomery Street coming in on the right side of the photo.

Darrell Heppner

Police Officer Ingram had dreamed yet again that the palace (Hotel), along with much of the city, had been destroyed by such a fire...On Tuesday, April 17, he decided to obtain personal protection for his home, destroyed though it would be according to his dream. He went to the Hartford Fire Insurance Company's office on California Street. There the company's Pacific agent, Adam Gillilard, drew up a two-thousand-dollar insurance policy on the Ingram home. With the policy safely signed and tucked away in his uniform pocket, he returned to duty...

The San Francisco Earthquake
By Gordon Thomas and Max Morgan Witts, 1971

Life was full for San Francisco on the Seventh (of April, 1906). It was happy bustling, wonderful time in those "innocent years" and spring weather marked the end of an overcast and rainy winter. Night approached with the cool breezes from the water that made San Francisco climate a joy...

The Earth Shook, The Sky Burned
By William Bronson, 1959

City Hall before the fire.

Darrell Heppner

San Francisco has violated all underwriting traditions and precedents by not burning up…

National Board of Fire Underwriters
October, 1905

The Government Mint before the fire.

San Francisco, serene,
Indifferent to Fate…
Bret Harte

Telegraph Hill before the fire.

Chapter Two:

The Earth in Agony

Darrell Heppner

Clock at Agnew's Insane Asylum stopped at the peak of the Earthquake's violence. Death and wreckage at the institution were unmatched anywhere in the earthquake zone. More than a hundred patients and keepers were killed in that terrible moment. The time recorded, 5:13 ½ AM, was probably not more than half a minute off. Exact clocks showed the onset to be a few seconds after 5:12 AM. Tremors built in intensity, paused, then returned with greatest surge of power. Total time: 65 to 72 seconds.

T. T Tourtillot

Wrecked houses after the earthquake.

Darrell Heppner

At 5:12 AM, Police Sergeant Jesse Cook stopped to chat with Al Levy, a young produce man, at the corner of Davis and Washington (streets). The clocks on the tower of the Ferry Building said that it was 5:15 AM – they were running a little fast. But it was to be months before those hands moved any farther, for at that instant, the earthquake struck.

The Earth Shook, The Sky Burned
By William Bronson, 1959

Ferry Building with Ferry Building Clock stopped at 5:16!

Darrell Heppner

From its very conception, the Palace Hotel had been designed to meet the two great natural hazards native to San Francisco: earthquake and fire. To guard against the former, the hotel had been built on a massive pillar foundation twelve feet deep. Its outer walls of brick were two feet thick. To give them even greater solidity, they had reinforced every four feet by double strips of iron bolted together…In the end three thousand tons of this reinforcing iron had been woven into the walls…

It is said in San Francisco that if the Palace ever burned down, the city itself would also be gutted.

The San Francisco Earthquake
By Gordon Thomas and Max Morgan Wits, 1971

The Palace Hotel before the fire.

Dame Nature appointed April 18, 1906, as housecleaning day for the "City Beautiful." Chinatown with its murdering thugs, highbinders and dens of vice was located in the very heart of the city and no power, civil or religious, could either reform or remove it. Nature did both in less than a minute.

The City Beautiful
Published by Houston & Harding
June 21,1906

Chintatown street scene.

Fallen columns at City Hall after the earthquake.

Darrell Heppner

Standing on Nob Hill, the home of the millionaires, it is perceived that the fire is no respecter of persons for when it has mowed down the thousands of acres south of Market it continued its destructive march on the north side, sweeping over Nob Hill laying every palace low, only the chimneys standing and they as spectral monuments to charred ruins…

The City Beautiful
Published by Houston & Harding
June 21,1906

Looking up Nob Hill after the fire.

Darrell Heppner

Fire Chief Dennis Sullivan was thinking about the 1905 report from the National Board of Fire Underwriters. It contained this startling statement:

"San Francisco has violated all underwriting precedents by not burning up. That it has not already done so is largely due to the vigilance of the Fire Department, which cannot be relied upon indefinitely to stave off the inevitable."

The San Francisco Earthquake
By Gordon Thomas Max Morgan Witts, 1971

City Hall after the quake.

The "sudden motion" was the result of stresses and strains which had accumulated miles below the ocean's surface, where the San Andreas Fault ran under the sea bed. The tremors had built up until one tectonic jolt one wall of the Fault slipped in one direction, the other the opposite way, grinding and thrusting and wrenching until finally the earth split open like a great wound…

The tremor was well on course, traveling at a speed of two miles per second…The earthquake struck ashore…It came out of the sea at seven thousand miles an hour…relentlessly the rip raced south…boring down on San Francisco, shifting billions of tons of earth, sending masses of rock rising and falling to form cliffs where only seconds before there was flat land.

With an energy greater than all the explosives used in World War II, the Fault had started its journey by smashing through the coast line of Humboldt County, two hundred miles north of San Francisco, demolishing whole forests of redwoods, bleak mountain spurs, and black shale bluffs…

The Unique Theatre, San Jose after the earthquake.

The rip sent out a shutter that wrecked the small town of Fort Bragg on the coast…following the scarred trails of other ancient fault breaks, it swept over peninsula uplands…in the process it wrecked the stone quadrangle of Stanford University at Palo Alto…in Salinas many buildings tumbled…in San Jose twenty one died from its effects…

In San Francisco, two people actually saw the earthquake. Jesse Cook, the police sergeant on duty in the produce market…years later Cook recalled: "There was a deep rumble, deep and terrible, and then I could see it actually coming up Washington Street. The whole street was undulating. It was as if the waves of the ocean were coming towards me, billowing, as they came."

The earth cracked open…the earth moved sideways…the earth moved up and down…on Union Street.

A few blocks away, John Barrett, the Examiner's city desk news editor, also saw and heard it approach, a long, low, moaning sound that set buildings "dancing" on their foundations. Suddenly he and his colleagues found themselves staggering. "It was as though the earth was slipping quietly away from under our feet. There was a sickening sway and we were all flat on our faces…

Newspaper Row before the fire.

Newspaper Row after the fire.

The Hearst Building after the earthquake and fire. You can clearly see the name chiseled into the stone

Then, slowly, the area south of Market Street began to move. Earth waves, two and three feet high, undulated through the ground, trembling foundations, rocking buildings, toppling towers and cornices.

Bent rails near the post office.

35

Cracks caused by the earthquake on Valencia Street.

Crack on Union Street from the earthquake.

The whole skyline was dancing, and it seemed that City Hall was leading the dance. At that moment seven million dollars worth of stone and brickwork was shaken off the administrative headquarters of San Francisco, leaving its frame standing among the shattered columns like a monstrous birdcage. Then the shaking stopped. Above the dust and rubble of falling masonry, the bell of Old St. Mary's Church still beat frantically, a harbinger of even worse devastation to come…

City hall was literally shaken apart.

Darrell Heppner

Ten whole seconds passed before the second phase of the tremor began…From outside came a sound like nails being wrenched out of the lid of a packing crate – and then the front of a building sprang outward and dropped to the ground. The same thing was happening all over the city.

Roofs were caving in, spreading their rafters. The rafters in turn kicked out the walls, collapsing buildings in a deafening roar. Thousands of brick chimneys crashed through ceilings…And through everything, the church bells jangled…

The San Francisco Earthquake
By Gordon Thomas and Max Morgan Witts, 1971

The Emporium Building after the earthquake.

Another view of The Emporium Building.

Mark Hopkins Hotel in ruins.

The Tivoli Theatre after the earthquake.

The Valencia Hotel, at 16th & Valencia, after the earthquake.

The Merchants Exchange after the earthquake.

Earthquake ruins south of Market Street.

The earthquake and fire did not distinguish between the rich and the poor.

The residence of W.H. Crocker lies in ruins.

The ruins of the A.N. Townes (Jownes) residence.
All that was left standing was this marble front portico, which is now safely housed in Golden Gate Park for all to admire.

Darrell Heppner

In the seventeen minutes following the earthquake, nearly fifty fires were reported in the downtown area of the City. Not one fire bell clanged. The Fire Department's central alarm system, housed in a building in Chinatown, had been wrecked…

The San Francisco Earthquake
By Gordon Thomas and Max Morgan Witts, 1971

Fire and smoke on Grant Avenue.

Fire and smoke at Market and Battery Streets.

Churches, which could have been a haven for comfort, were not spared.

Outside of Memorial Chapel at Stanford after the earthquake.

Inside of Memorial Chapel at Stanford after the earthquake.

St. Dominic's Church earthquake damage.

Another view of St. Dominic's with the unique earthquake damage to its bell tower.

Weler Church after the fire.

St. Patrick's Church and the Scott Van Arsdell Building.

North, south, east and west. From every direction, in every direction – there was devastation.
It was not possible to find a piece of the city that was not touched, damaged or destroyed.

Montgomery Street looking north from Sutter Street

No. 43. City South East from California St. Hill
Copyrighted 1906. by R.J. Waters & Co.

Looking south from California Street Hill.

Looking south from Telegraph Hill.

The Ferry Building in the distance looking down California Street to the east.

Powell and Post Streets looking east.

A very dismal sight looking east from 6th Street to Market Street.

A view of the earthquake damage from Pine and Kearny Streets looking east.

Total annihilation of buildings on California as viewed looking east from Stockton Street.

California Street Hill viewed from the Merchants Exchange Building on California Street, looking west.

Burn district viewed from Fremont and Mission Streets looking northwest.

Even though the damage to buildings and property was devastating; there was also the human element to be considered. The damage was so widespread that it took a while for any kind of aid to become available.

Golden Gate Park Playground before the earthquake and fire.

No.129. Refugee Camp Golden Gate Park.

R.J.Waters & Co.

Golden Gate Park with the refugee camp after the earthquake.

Interior of one of the soup kitchens.

Refugees fleeing fire and camping out.

A street kitchen.

Distributing food and clothing for the needy.

Bread line at Geary & Webster.

All that was saved by a resident on Van Ness Avenue.

Jefferson Square relief and refugees from the quake.

Fleeing from the fire.

A homeless woman cooking on the street.

No. 105. Hall of Justice Portsmouth Square

R.J. Waters? Co.

The Hall of Justice and Portsmouth Square with permanent visitors; note the tents.

Burn district viewed from 21st and Valencia; again, note the tents on the lawn.

Removing the dead.

Chapter Three

More…

More evidence of the massive destruction of the earthquake. The entire city resembled a war zone.

The Masonic Temple after the earthquake.

The Call Building, the Annex and the Hamm Building after the earthquake. The Call Building, actually the Claus Spreckels Building (sugar empire), was known by the morning newspaper which was published there.

California and Kearny Streets after the earthquake.

Kohler & Chase Building at Post and Kearny Streets.

The Chronicle, Mutual Savings Bank and Call Buildings.

A devastative bombed out look from Pine and Powell streets.

Lick House entrance, Bullock & Jones and San Francisco Savings Bank Buildings.

Crossley Building at New Montgomery and Mission Streets.

Nevada Bank.

First National Bank.

Mission Street between 3rd and 4th Streets.

Pacific Mutual and Italian American Bank Buildings.

Chapter Four

Before and After

The Ferry Building before the earthquake.

The Ferry Building after the earthquake and fire.

Looking down Market Street before the earthquake and fire.

Looking down Market Street after the earthquake and fire.

103

Market Street looking east from 5th Street before the earthquake.

Market Street during the fire.

Panoramic view from Nob Hill before the fire.

Panoramic view from Nob Hill after the fire.

YMCA before the fire.

YMCA after the fire.

The Emporium before the fire.

The Emporium after the fire.

The Palace Hotel before the fire and earthquake.

The Palace Hotel after the fire and earthquake.

The beautiful interior of the Palace Hotel before the fire and earthquake.

The Palace Hotel after the fire and earthquake.

City Hall before the earthquake and fire.

City Hall after the earthquake and fire.

Telegraph Hill before the earthquake and fire.

Telegraph Hill after the earthquake and fire.

Newspaper Row before the fire.

Newspaper Row after the fire.

121

Looking up Sacramento Street before the earthquake and fire.

Looking down Sacramento Street during the fire.

123

Chapter Five

Rising Out of the Ashes

Construction and Re-construction

Looking down Market Street a year later (May of 1907).

Rebuilding at Kearny and Geary Streets four months later (August of 1906).

Workmen at lunch.

The Temporary St. Francis Hotel

San Andreas Fault (1906 Break)

San Francisco Fire

Starting point of major fires
Course of fires
First day
Second day
Third and fourth days
Area of fire

1. Post Office
2. Emporium
3. Call Building
4. Palace Hotel
5. Flood Building
6. St. Francis Hotel
7. Union Square
8. Mills Building
9. Merchants Exchange
10. Fairmont Hotel
11. Portsmouth Square
12. Hall of Justice
13. Monkey Block
14. Appraisers' Building
15. "House of the Flag"
16. Lafayette Park
17. City Hall
18. Ferry Building
19. Mission Delores
20. Old St. Mary's Church
21. U.S. Mint